X-TREME FACTS: SPACE

THE INTERNATIONAL SPACE STATION

by Catherine C. Finan

BEARPORT
PUBLISHING

Minneapolis, Minnesota

Credits:

Cover, Janis Abolins/Shutterstock, robert_s/Shutterstock, Yurij Omelchenko/Shutterstock, Alter-ego/Shutterstock, Klever_ok/Shutterstock; Title Page, 4 bottom, 5 top, 5 middle, 7 top, 7 bottom, 8, 9 top, 9 bottom, 10 top, 11 top, 12, 14 top, 14 bottom, 15 top, 16, 17 middle, 17 bottom, 18, 19, 20, 21 top, 22, 23 bottom, 24, 25 bottom, 26 top, 27 bottom, 28 left, NASA/Public Domain; 4 top, 6–7 bottom, NASA/Roscosmos/Public Domain; 5 bottom, NASA/GCTC/Andrey Shelepin/Public Domain; 9 middle, Jukka Risikko/Shutterstock; 10 bottom left, Elena Nichizhenova/Shutterstock; 10 bottom right, Nanette Dreyer/Shutterstock; 11 middle, Mil.ru/Creative Commons; 11 bottom left, NASA/Joel Kowsky/Public Domain; 13 bottom, NASA/Joseph M. Acaba/Public Domain; 15 bottom, Gzzz/Creative Commons; 15 bottom left, 15 bottom right, 23 top, NASA/Robert Markowitz/Public Domain; 21 Matthew Clemente/Shutterstock; 21 bottom right, Jacek Chabraszewski/Shutterstock; 22 bottom right, Josep Curto/Shutterstock; 25 top, SpaceX/NASA/Public Domain; 26 bottom, Musker Busker/Creative Commons; 26 middle left, 26 middle right, Merlin74/Shutterstock; 27 top right, FrameStockFootages/Shutterstock; 27 bottom left, Kuznetsov Dmitriy/Shutterstock; 28 bottom right, Kozak Sergii/Shutterstock, PHILIPIMAGE/Shutterstock; 13 middle, 28–29, Austen Photography

President: Jen Jenson
Director of Product Development: Spencer Brinker
Senior Editor: Allison Juda
Associate Editor: Charly Haley
Designer: Elena Klinkner

Developed and produced for Bearport Publishing by BlueAppleWorks Inc.
Managing Editor for BlueAppleWorks: Melissa McClellan
Art Director: T.J. Choleva
Photo Research: Jane Reid

Library of Congress Cataloging-in-Publication Data

Names: Finan, Catherine C., 1972- author.
Title: The International Space Station / by Catherine C. Finan.
Description: Minneapolis, Minnesota : Bearport Publishing, [2022] | Series: X-treme facts: space | Includes bibliographical references and index.
Identifiers: LCCN 2021026696 (print) | LCCN 2021026697 (ebook) | ISBN 9781636915074 (library binding) | ISBN 9781636915142 (paperback) | ISBN 9781636915210 (ebook)
Subjects: LCSH: International Space Station--Juvenile literature. | Space stations--Juvenile literature. | Life support systems (Space environment)--Juvenile literature.
Classification: LCC TL797.15 .F56 2022 (print) | LCC TL797.15 (ebook) | DDC 629.44/2--dc23
LC record available at https://lccn.loc.gov/2021026696
LC ebook record available at https://lccn.loc.gov/2021026697

Copyright © 2022 Bearport Publishing Company. All rights reserved. No part of this publication may be reproduced in whole or in part, stored in any retrieval system, or transmitted in any form or by any means, electronic, mechanical, photocopying, recording, or otherwise, without written permission from the publisher.

For more information, write to Bearport Publishing, 5357 Penn Avenue South, Minneapolis, MN 55419.
Printed in the United States of America.

Contents

The Incredible ISS 4
Building a Space Station 6
Around the World in 90 Minutes 8
Meet the Crew 10
Just Another Day on the ISS 12
Get to Work! 14
Space Stroll, Anyone? 16
Extreme Outfits 18
Toilet Talk 20
Your Body Aboard the ISS 22
Just Dropping By 24
From the ISS to Mars! 26

ISS Model 28
Glossary 30
Read More 31
Learn More Online 31
Index 32
About the Author 32

The Incredible ISS

Look up into a clear sky around dawn or dusk, and you might see something incredible. At first glance, the spot of bright light looks like a star. But it moves steadily across the sky. What is it? An alien **spacecraft**? Nope. It's the **International** Space Station, or ISS. The ISS is about 250 miles (400 km) above our heads, **orbiting** around Earth. And what's even more incredible is that a team of people lives inside it!

The ISS's main purpose is **research**. Imagine doing science experiments **while floating above Earth!**

THE VIEW IS OUTTA THIS WORLD!

THAT'S RIGHT! IT HAD ONLY THREE ROOMS.

THE ISS WAS SO TINY BACK THEN!

The first crew to live aboard the ISS **arrived there more than 20 years ago.**

Building a Space Station

So, how do you build a huge floating home and **laboratory** in space? With lots of careful planning! Starting in 1998, there were 42 flights from Earth to space to deliver parts for the ISS's main structure. Astronauts had to put all the parts together. Today, the ISS is the largest human-made space object. It's also the most expensive structure ever built, costing $120 billion. What did they get for all that money?

The ISS has six sleeping areas for the crew—**but only two bathrooms.**

I CALL DIBS ON THE BATHROOM!

BETTER GET IN LINE!

The ISS weighs 420 tons (381 t). That's **about the same as 350 cars.**

Around the World in 90 Minutes

You might think something as huge and heavy as the ISS couldn't possibly move very fast—but you'd be wrong! The space station travels at about 5 miles per second (8 kps). That's about 18,000 miles per hour (29,000 kph). At that incredible speed, the ISS orbits Earth in just 90 minutes!

In one day's worth of orbiting, the ISS travels about the distance from Earth to the moon and back.

THAT'S THE MOST BEAUTIFUL SUNSET I'VE SEEN SINCE . . . OH, ABOUT 90 MINUTES AGO!

A person aboard the ISS sees a sunrise and sunset each time the space station orbits Earth. In just 24 hours, they would see 16 sunrises and sunsets!

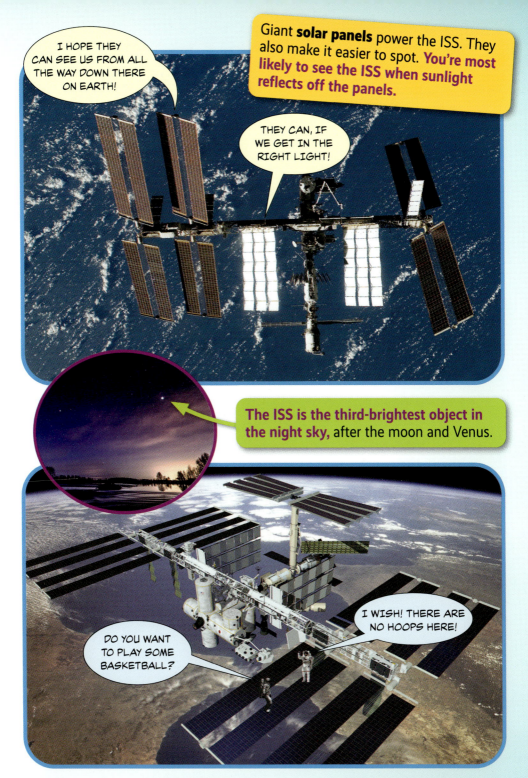

If you put all of the ISS's solar panels together, they could cover eight basketball courts.

Meet the Crew

The ISS is called the International Space Station for good reason. The station was planned and built by nations around the world—and its crew is international, too! The ISS typically has a live-in crew of six people from different countries. Throughout the station's history, more than 240 astronauts from 19 countries have visited, lived, and worked there. What does it take to be part of the ISS crew?

Crewmembers go through extreme training to get ready for their time on the ISS. Practicing deep underwater prepares them for working in low **gravity**.

ISS crewmembers need to learn Russian so they can talk to the Russian Mission Control Center.

THIS TRAINING IS NO DAY AT THE BEACH, LET ME TELL YA.

LEARNING RUSSIAN WON'T BE EASY EITHER!

OH, HE'LL BE FINE. ASTRONAUTS ARE VERY SMART!

10

Just Another Day on the ISS

Being an ISS crewmember is exciting, but it's also challenging. The crew has to adjust to life in low gravity, which makes everyday tasks more difficult. You have to get used to floating from place to place instead of walking. Eating dinner can be frustrating when your food is floating away from you! And how do you sleep if you can't lie down? Luckily, the ISS is made to overcome these challenges.

Crewmembers must exercise for at least two hours each day to stay healthy.

C'MON, PUT YOUR STRAPS ON AND RUN WITH ME!

NAH, I FEEL LIKE AIR-SWIMMING TODAY!

The ISS's treadmill has straps to keep people from floating away!

Get to Work!

After a (hopefully) restful sleep strapped to a wall high above Earth, the ISS crew gets to work. They look at changes in Earth's **atmosphere** and experiment with things such as growing vegetables in space. The main goal of their experiments is to learn how space affects different things. This information will be used for future space exploration.

The crew also has to repair the ISS so it can run safely. Talk about a full workday!

A workday on the ISS lasts from 6:00 a.m. to 9:30 p.m.

ISS crewmembers have successfully grown salad greens, radishes, and potatoes.

The ISS crew has studied more than 100 billion **space particles**. This might help us better understand how the universe began!

Crewmembers are also studied! Learning about the effects of space on the human body may help us safely travel farther into space in the future.

A yearlong experiment on twin astronauts **Scott and Mark Kelly** showed space's effects on crewmember Scott compared to Mark on Earth.

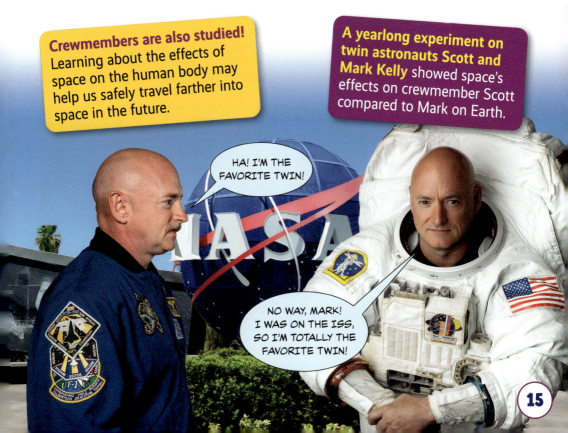

Space Stroll, Anyone?

Imagine heading out into space with only a few strong ropes to keep you from floating away. Sounds scary *and* cool, right? Luckily, the ISS crew knows how to stay safe while working outside the station on spacewalks. Crewmembers go on spacewalks to test how space affects different things. They also do spacewalks to make repairs to the ISS as well as other spacecraft and **satellites**. Let's take a space stroll . . .

Crewmembers leave the ISS through an airlock. They go through one door, lock it behind them, then open another door into space!

THIS AIRLOCK IS A BIT OF A TIGHT SQUEEZE!

DON'T WORRY, YOU'LL BE OUT IN SPACE SOON!

Since December 1998, ISS crewmembers have taken more than 230 spacewalks!

Extreme Outfits

If you're going on a spacewalk, you'll need the right outfit! ISS crewmembers wear the latest in spacesuit **technology** to venture outside the station. If they didn't, they'd be in big trouble! The spacewalk spacesuit, or Extravehicular Mobility Unit (EMU), is like a mini spaceship for your body. It protects you from the dangers of space. Without it, extreme temperatures, **radiation**, dust, and space **debris** would be deadly. Time to suit up!

An astronaut puts on a spacesuit hours before a spacewalk. **Oxygen** inside the suit gets their body ready to be outside the ISS.

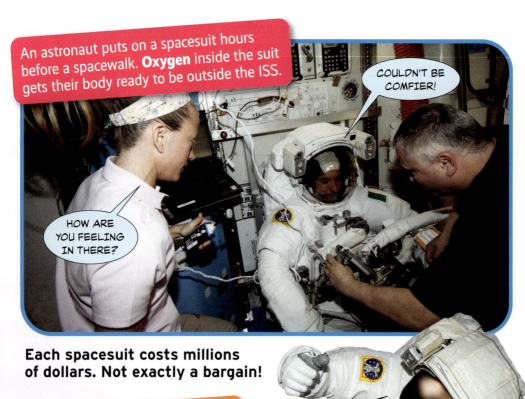

COULDN'T BE COMFIER!

HOW ARE YOU FEELING IN THERE?

Each spacesuit costs millions of dollars. Not exactly a bargain!

No spacesuit is complete without the Maximum Absorption Garment, a special diaper for peeing and pooping during spacewalks.

WHEN YOU GOTTA GO, YOU GOTTA GO!

The jet pack's thrusters are controlled by a joystick, just like a video game!

EMU gloves have mini heaters built in! This keeps crewmembers' fingers warm so they can grab tools.

The EMU can keep astronauts safe in temperatures that range from −250°F (−157°C) to 250°F (121°C).

Underneath the EMU's outer suit is a stretchy suit with 300 ft (91 m) of tubes. Cold water flows through the tubes to keep astronauts cool.

19

Toilet Talk

A person has to pee and poop, even in space! Spacewalking astronauts rely on Maximum Absorption Garments, but what's the toilet situation inside the ISS? On Earth, gravity pulls pee and poop down and away from you. In space's low gravity, we need some help. Crewmembers on the ISS pee into a funnel that sucks liquid away. Special toilets suction poop away so it doesn't float around—*ew!* And after that, the pee and poop still have more to do.

There's not enough room on the ISS to store drinking water. **So, about 85 percent of crewmembers' pee is recycled into water they drink later!**

Your Body Aboard the ISS

Living on the ISS certainly affects bodily functions such as peeing and pooping, but it also affects people's actual bodies in some pretty major ways. Low gravity causes people to lose bone and muscle strength. Without gravity pulling body fluids downward, crewmembers develop big upper bodies and skinny legs—a condition affectionately known as chicken leg syndrome. Body fluids traveling upward also cause people's faces to swell. What else might happen to your body aboard the ISS?

People get a little taller in space! This is because low gravity makes the body's joints spread out, and fluid fills these spaces.

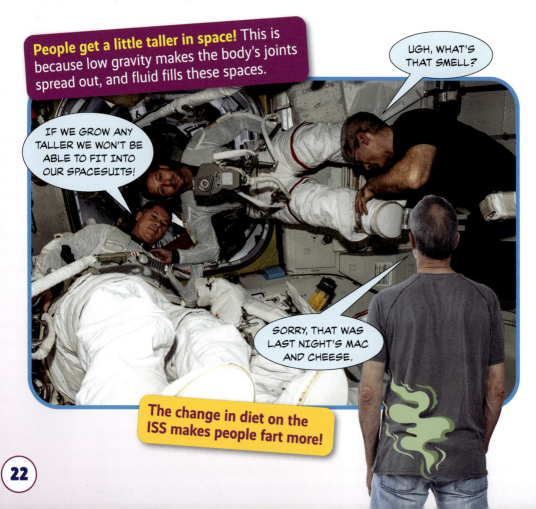

IF WE GROW ANY TALLER WE WON'T BE ABLE TO FIT INTO OUR SPACESUITS!

UGH, WHAT'S THAT SMELL?

SORRY, THAT WAS LAST NIGHT'S MAC AND CHEESE.

The change in diet on the ISS makes people fart more!

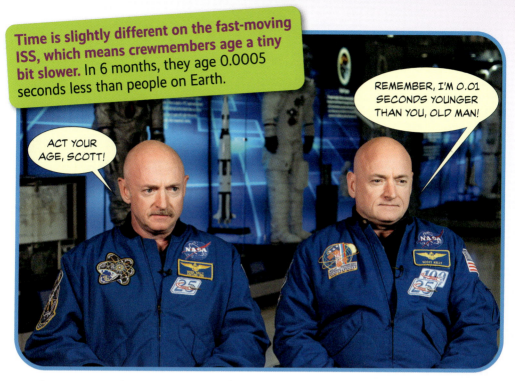

After Scott Kelly's year aboard the ISS, he'd aged 0.01 seconds less than his twin brother Mark on Earth.

Just Dropping By

It might seem like the ISS wouldn't hit much traffic on its orbit high above Earth. But there's actually a lot of action up there! The ISS can carry only so many meals, scientific supplies, and other items necessary for life in space. Spacecraft from Earth arrive regularly to keep the station stocked. Who might drop by?

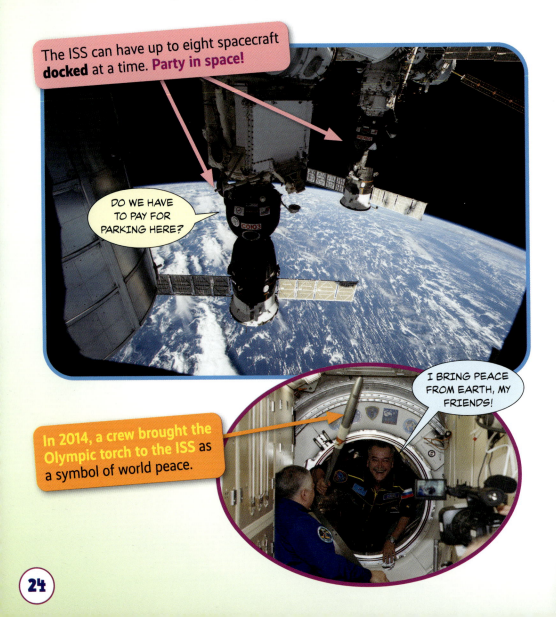

The ISS can have up to eight spacecraft **docked** at a time. **Party in space!**

DO WE HAVE TO PAY FOR PARKING HERE?

In 2014, a crew brought the Olympic torch to the ISS as a symbol of world peace.

I BRING PEACE FROM EARTH, MY FRIENDS!

24

The company SpaceX's Dragon spacecraft can carry 13,000 pounds (6,000 kg) of supplies to the ISS per trip.

From the ISS to Mars!

Living on the ISS is extreme. But what about traveling farther? Much of the ISS's research is about space travel in the future, and the next stop is Mars! Astronauts may make a trip to Mars as early as the 2030s. And when they do, the ISS's research will be an important part of getting that crew to Mars safely. Maybe you'll be one of the first people to set foot on Mars!

Technology for the Mars mission will first be tested on the moon, using research from ISS experiments.

THIS IS GETTING OLD. I CAN'T WAIT TO MOVE ON TO MARS!

WATCH OUT, MARS! HERE WE COME!

ARE WE THERE YET?

A mission to Mars would take two years! This includes travel time to and from Mars as well as time on its surface. That's a long trip!

It takes 0.001 seconds for a message to travel from Earth to the ISS. The same message would take 12.5 minutes to reach Mars.

Someday, people might even live on Mars. We can thank the brave crewmembers of the ISS for making it possible!

ISS Model
Craft Project

Have you ever dreamed of going to space? Now that you know what you might be in for, do you think you'd want to live and work on the ISS? You could become part of the crew someday. But until then, you can build your own ISS model! Piece it together like the real space station.

What You Will Need
- Scissors
- Silver cardstock
- Glue or tape
- Four wooden skewers
- Aluminum foil
- A black marker

The ISS is made up of hundreds of parts.

Step One

Use scissors to cut one rectangle 6.5 in. by 12 in. (16.5 cm x 30.5 cm) and another rectangle 5.5 in. by 7 in. (14 cm x 17.75 cm) from the silver cardstock. Then, cut 8 pieces of aluminum foil 3 in. by 4.5 in. (7.5 cm x 11.5 cm) each.

Step Two

Fold ½ in. (1.3 cm) from the edge of one long side of the larger piece of silver cardstock. Keeping the flap bent inward, fold the rectangle in half lengthwise. Then, fold it in half lengthwise a second time. You will have four equal sides, plus a flap for glue. Fold all the aluminum foil pieces in half, lengthwise.

Step Three

Put glue along the folded flap and press it to the other side to make a rectangular tube. Put glue along the long edge of the smaller piece of cardstock and roll it into a cylinder, sticking the long edges together.

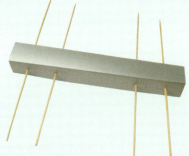

Step Four

Push two wooden skewers through the side of each end of the rectangular tube.

Step Five

Open one foil piece and add glue to one side. Center the foil at the end of one skewer and fold together. Repeat for the other seven pieces. Glue or tape the cylinder to the long rectanglar base in the center. Decorate with the black marker.

atmosphere the gases surrounding Earth

debris pieces of something that has been broken or destroyed

docked linked with another spacecraft while in space

gravity the force that pulls things toward Earth, the sun, or other large objects in space

international involving two or more countries

laboratory a place used for scientific experiments

orbiting moving in a regular path around another object, usually in space; the path is also called an orbit

oxygen a colorless, odorless gas people need to live

radiation a type of energy that can be dangerous to humans

research information collected through experiments or other studies

satellites bodies in space that orbit objects of larger size

solar panels flat boards made up of cells that convert sunlight to energy

spacecraft a vehicle designed to travel in space

space particles dust and other very tiny things found in space

technology the use of science and engineering to invent useful tools or to solve problems

Read More

Lawrence, Ellen. *Working in Space (Space-ology).* New York: Bearport Publishing, 2019.

Rechner, Amy. *Astronaut (Torque: Cool Careers).* Minneapolis: Bellwether Media, 2020.

Rose, Rachel. *Christina Koch: Astronaut and Engineer (Bearport Biographies).* Minneapolis: Bearport Publishing, 2021.

Learn More Online

1. Go to **www.factsurfer.com** or scan the QR code below.

2. Enter **"ISS"** into the search box.

3. Click on the cover of this book to see a list of websites.

Index

exercise 12

experiments 4, 14–15, 26

Extravehicular Mobility Unit (EMU) 18–19

food 12–13

gravity 10, 12, 20, 22–23

Kelly, Scott 15, 23

Koch, Christina 11, 17

Mars 26–27

Maximum Absorption Garment 18, 20

Meir, Jessica 17

moon 8–9, 26

orbit 4, 8, 24

Polyakov, Valeri 11

research 4, 26

sleeping 6, 12–14

solar panels 9

Solovyev, Anatoly 17

spacesuits 17–18, 22

spacewalk 16–20

SpaceX 25

toilets 20–21

Whitson, Peggy 11

About the Author

Catherine C. Finan is a writer living in northeastern Pennsylvania. One of her most-prized possessions is a telescope that lets her peer into space.